THE JOURNAL

52 Weeks of Self-Discovery

Julie Adams

© 2025 Spiritbuilding Publishers.

All rights reserved. No part of this book may be reproduced in any form without the written permission of the publisher.

Published by
Spiritbuilding Publishers
9700 Ferry Road, Waynesville, OH 45068

The Journal: 52 Weeks to Self-Discovery
by Julie Adams

ISBN: 9781964805122

spiritbuilding.com

THE JOURNAL
HOW TO USE

Thank you for wanting to explore new ways to journal. If you're like me, I struggle to know what to do with journaling and how it applies to my life. The goal should be a Discovery of You!. This is a word study designed to help with daily life along with spiritual life. The desire to improve our lives can be accomplished with one single word.

Each week will be a word to explore. Included is a search for biblical application, women in the Bible who exemplified the word, how the word was seen in your week, if you practiced it, should have or saw it personified.

At the end of each week is a page called Snapshot. You can write about your word, draw about it or paste a photo as a reminder. Remember, journaling is about awareness of self, reflection, honesty and capturing the transformation of you!

It is possible you have never done anything like this before, and that's okay. A deeper understanding of words, your spiritual knowledge and application, along with your own spiritual well-being, helps develop connection of culture and context. Enrich your study by learning what a Greek or Hebrew word meant when written and the how modern day translations may be di erent.

Enjoy journaling and learning and make it unique to you!

All my best,

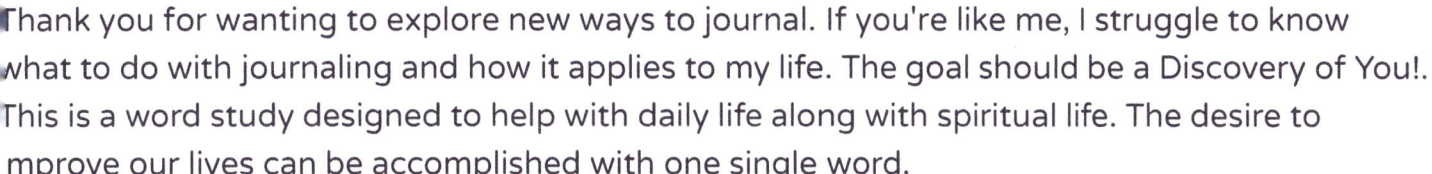

Julie Adams

WWW.STILLWATERSLIFE.COM
julie@stillwaterslife.com

Week 1...
Loyalty

My Definition **Bible Examples**

- ☐ I saw loyalty personified
- ☐ I need to work on this
- ☐ This week I nailed it!

- ☐ Women in the Bible
- ☐ My favorite
- ☐ Bible verses

Snapshot of My Week

Week 2 ...
Trust

My Definition

Bible Examples

- ☐ I saw trust personified
- ☐ I need to work on this
- ☐ This week I nailed it!

- ☐ Women in the Bible
- ☐ My favorite
- ☐ Bible verses

Snapshot of My Week

Week 3 ...
Fear

My Definition

Bible Examples

- ☐ I saw fear personified
- ☐ I need to work on this
- ☐ This week I nailed it!

- ☐ Women in the Bible
- ☐ My favorite
- ☐ Bible verses

Snapshot of My Week

Week 4 ...
Grief

My Definition | **Bible Examples**

- ☐ I saw grief personified
- ☐ I need to work on this
- ☐ This week I nailed it!

- ☐ Women in the Bible
- ☐ My favorite
- ☐ Bible verses

Snapshot of My Week

Week 5 ...

Joy

My Definition　　　　　　　　　　　　　　　　Bible Examples

- ☐ I saw joy personified
- ☐ I need to work on this
- ☐ This week I nailed it!

- ☐ Women in the Bible
- ☐ My favorite
- ☐ Bible verses

Snapshot of My Week

Week 6 ...
Peace

My Definition

Bible Examples

- ☐ I saw peace personified
- ☐ I need to work on this
- ☐ This week I nailed it!

- ☐ Women in the Bible
- ☐ My favorite
- ☐ Bible verses

Snapshot of My Week

Week 7 ...
Anxiety

My Definition

Bible Examples

- ☐ I saw anxiety personified
- ☐ I need to work on this
- ☐ This week I nailed it!

- ☐ Women in the Bible
- ☐ My favorite
- ☐ Bible verses

Snapshot of My Week

Week 8 ...
Prayer

My Definition

Bible Examples

- ☐ I saw prayer personified
- ☐ I need to work on this
- ☐ This week I nailed it!

- ☐ Women in the Bible
- ☐ My favorite
- ☐ Bible verses

Snapshot of My Week

Week 9 ...
Repentance

My Definition

Bible Examples

- ☐ I saw repentance personified
- ☐ I need to work on this
- ☐ This week I nailed it!

- ☐ Women in the Bible
- ☐ My favorite
- ☐ Bible verses

Snapshot of My Week

Week 10...
Forgiveness

My Definition

Bible Examples

- ☐ I saw forgiveness personified
- ☐ I need to work on this
- ☐ This week I nailed it!

- ☐ Women in the Bible
- ☐ My favorite
- ☐ Bible verses

Snapshot of My Week

Week 11...
Humility

My Definition

Bible Examples

- ☐ I saw humility personified
- ☐ Women in the Bible
- ☐ I need to work on this
- ☐ My favorite
- ☐ This week I nailed it!
- ☐ Bible verses

Snapshot of My Week

Snapshot of My Week

Week 12 ...
Contentment

My Definition

Bible Examples

- ☐ I saw contentment personified
- ☐ I need to work on this
- ☐ This week I nailed it!

- ☐ Women in the Bible
- ☐ My favorite
- ☐ Bible verses

Snapshot of My Week

Week 13...
Frustration

My Definition

Bible Examples

- ☐ I saw frustration personified
- ☐ I need to work on this
- ☐ This week I nailed it!
- ☐ Women in the Bible
- ☐ My favorite
- ☐ Bible verses

Snapshot of My Week

Week 14...
Anger

My Definition 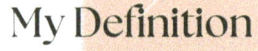 **Bible Examples**

- ☐ I saw anger personified
- ☐ I need to work on this
- ☐ This week I nailed it!

- ☐ Women in the Bible
- ☐ My favorite
- ☐ Bible verses

Snapshot of My Week

_____

Week 15...

Hope

My Definition

Bible Examples

- ☐ I saw hope personified
- ☐ I need to work on this
- ☐ This week I nailed it!
- ☐ Women in the Bible
- ☐ My favorite
- ☐ Bible verses

Snapshot of My Week

Week 16...
Goodness

My Definition

Bible Examples

- [ ] I saw goodness personified
- [ ] I need to work on this
- [ ] This week I nailed it!

- [ ] Women in the Bible
- [ ] My favorite
- [ ] Bible verses

Snapshot of My Week

Week 17...

Kindness

My Definition

Bible Examples

- ☐ I saw kindness personified
- ☐ I need to work on this
- ☐ This week I nailed it!
- ☐ Women in the Bible
- ☐ My favorite
- ☐ Bible verses

Snapshot of My Week

___

Week 18 ...
Shame

My Definition   **Bible Examples**

- ☐ I saw shame personified
- ☐ I need to work on this
- ☐ This week I nailed it!
- ☐ Women in the Bible
- ☐ My favorite
- ☐ Bible verses

Snapshot of My Week

Week 19...
Sacrifice

My Definition

Bible Examples

- ☐ I saw sacrifice personified
- ☐ I need to work on this
- ☐ This week I nailed it!
- ☐ Women in the Bible
- ☐ My favorite
- ☐ Bible verses

Snapshot of My Week

Week 20...
Compassion

My Definition

Bible Examples

- ☐ I saw compassion personified
- ☐ I need to work on this
- ☐ This week I nailed it!
- ☐ Women in the Bible
- ☐ My favorite
- ☐ Bible verses

Snapshot of My Week

———

Week 21...
Mindfulness

My Definition

Bible Examples

- ☐ I saw mindfulness personified
- ☐ I need to work on this
- ☐ This week I nailed it!

- ☐ Women in the Bible
- ☐ My favorite
- ☐ Bible verses

Snapshot of My Week

———————

Week 22...
Honor

My Definition 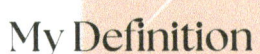 **Bible Examples**

- ☐ I saw honor personified
- ☐ I need to work on this
- ☐ This week I nailed it!

- ☐ Women in the Bible
- ☐ My favorite
- ☐ Bible verses

Snapshot of My Week

Week 23...

Pain

My Definition

Bible Examples

- ☐ I saw pain personified
- ☐ I need to work on this
- ☐ This week I nailed it!

- ☐ Women in the Bible
- ☐ My favorite
- ☐ Bible verses

Snapshot of My Week

Week 24 ...
Healing

My Definition

Bible Examples

- ☐ I saw healing personified
- ☐ I need to work on this
- ☐ This week I nailed it!

- ☐ Women in the Bible
- ☐ My favorite
- ☐ Bible verses

Snapshot of My Week

———————————

Week 25...
Worship

My Definition

Bible Examples

- ☐ I saw worship personified
- ☐ I need to work on this
- ☐ This week I nailed it!

- ☐ Women in the Bible
- ☐ My favorite
- ☐ Bible verses

Snapshot of My Week

Week 26 ...
Pure

My Definition **Bible Examples**

- ☐ I saw pure personified
- ☐ I need to work on this
- ☐ This week I nailed it!

- ☐ Women in the Bible
- ☐ My favorite
- ☐ Bible verses

Snapshot of My Week

Week 27 ...
Lonely

My Definition

Bible Examples

- ☐ I saw lonely personified
- ☐ I need to work on this
- ☐ This week I nailed it!

- ☐ Women in the Bible
- ☐ My favorite
- ☐ Bible verses

Snapshot of My Week

Week 28 ...
Grace

My Definition **Bible Examples**

- ☐ I saw grace personified
- ☐ I need to work on this
- ☐ This week I nailed it!

- ☐ Women in the Bible
- ☐ My favorite
- ☐ Bible verses

Snapshot of My Week

Week 29 ... Compromise

My Definition   **Bible Examples**

- ☐ I saw compromise personified
- ☐ I need to work on this
- ☐ This week I nailed it!
- ☐ Women in the Bible
- ☐ My favorite
- ☐ Bible verses

Snapshot of My Week

Week 30 ...
Lying

My Definition   **Bible Examples**

- ☐ I saw lying personified
- ☐ I need to work on this
- ☐ This week I nailed it!

- ☐ Women in the Bible
- ☐ My favorite
- ☐ Bible verses

Snapshot of My Week

Week 31...
Patience

My Definition

Bible Examples

- ☐ I saw patience personified
- ☐ I need to work on this
- ☐ This week I nailed it!

- ☐ Women in the Bible
- ☐ My favorite
- ☐ Bible verses

Snapshot of My Week

———————

Week 32 ...
Greed

My Definition

Bible Examples

- ☐ I saw greed personified
- ☐ I need to work on this
- ☐ This week I nailed it!

- ☐ Women in the Bible
- ☐ My favorite
- ☐ Bible verses

Snapshot of My Week

Week 33 ...

Safe

My Definition

Bible Examples

- ☐ I saw safe personified
- ☐ I need to work on this
- ☐ This week I nailed it!

- ☐ Women in the Bible
- ☐ My favorite
- ☐ Bible verses

Snapshot of My Week

Week 34 ...
Strength

My Definition

Bible Examples

- ☐ I saw strength personified
- ☐ I need to work on this
- ☐ This week I nailed it!
- ☐ Women in the Bible
- ☐ My favorite
- ☐ Bible verses

Snapshot of My Week

Week 35 ...
Trials

My Definition  **Bible Examples**

- ☐ I saw trials personified
- ☐ I need to work on this
- ☐ This week I nailed it!

- ☐ Women in the Bible
- ☐ My favorite
- ☐ Bible verses

Snapshot of My Week

Week 36 ...
Complaining

My Definition

Bible Examples

- ☐ I saw complaining personified
- ☐ I need to work on this
- ☐ This week I nailed it!

- ☐ Women in the Bible
- ☐ My favorite
- ☐ Bible verses

Snapshot of My Week

Week 37 ...
Confidential

My Definition **Bible Examples**

- ☐ I saw confidential personified
- ☐ I need to work on this
- ☐ This week I nailed it!

- ☐ Women in the Bible
- ☐ My favorite
- ☐ Bible verses

Snapshot of My Week

Week 38...
Gossip

My Definition

Bible Examples

- ☐ I saw gossip personified
- ☐ I need to work on this
- ☐ This week I nailed it!
- ☐ Women in the Bible
- ☐ My favorite
- ☐ Bible verses

Snapshot of My Week

___

Week 39 ...
Heaven

My Definition

Bible Examples

- ☐ I saw heaven personified
- ☐ Women in the Bible
- ☐ I need to work on this
- ☐ My favorite
- ☐ This week I nailed it!
- ☐ Bible verses

Snapshot of My Week

Week 40 ...
Trauma

My Definition

Bible Examples

- ☐ I saw trauma personified
- ☐ I need to work on this
- ☐ This week I nailed it!

- ☐ Women in the Bible
- ☐ My favorite
- ☐ Bible verses

Snapshot of My Week

Week 41...
Morality

My Definition **Bible Examples**

- ☐ I saw morality personified
- ☐ I need to work on this
- ☐ This week I nailed it!

- ☐ Women in the Bible
- ☐ My favorite
- ☐ Bible verses

Snapshot of My Week

Week 42 ...
Purpose

My Definition

Bible Examples

- ☐ I saw purpose personified
- ☐ I need to work on this
- ☐ This week I nailed it!
- ☐ Women in the Bible
- ☐ My favorite
- ☐ Bible verses

Snapshot of My Week

Week 43...
Fragmented

My Definition

Bible Examples

- ☐ I saw fragmented personified
- ☐ I need to work on this
- ☐ This week I nailed it!
- ☐ Women in the Bible
- ☐ My favorite
- ☐ Bible verses

Snapshot of My Week

Week 44 ...
Rescue

My Definition

Bible Examples

- ☐ I saw rescue personified
- ☐ I need to work on this
- ☐ This week I nailed it!

- ☐ Women in the Bible
- ☐ My favorite
- ☐ Bible verses

Snapshot of My Week

Week 45 ...
Betrayal

My Definition

Bible Examples

- ☐ I saw betrayal personified
- ☐ I need to work on this
- ☐ This week I nailed it!

- ☐ Women in the Bible
- ☐ My favorite
- ☐ Bible verses

Snapshot of My Week

Week 46 ...
Warrior

My Definition **Bible Examples**

- ☐ I saw warrior personified
- ☐ I need to work on this
- ☐ This week I nailed it!

- ☐ Women in the Bible
- ☐ My favorite
- ☐ Bible verses

Snapshot of My Week

Week 47 ...

Enemy

My Definition

Bible Examples

- ☐ I saw enemy personified
- ☐ I need to work on this
- ☐ This week I nailed it!
- ☐ Women in the Bible
- ☐ My favorite
- ☐ Bible verses

Snapshot of My Week

Week 48 ...
Transformation

My Definition

Bible Examples

- ☐ I saw transformation personified
- ☐ I need to work on this
- ☐ This week I nailed it!

- ☐ Women in the Bible
- ☐ My favorite
- ☐ Bible verses

Snapshot of My Week

Week 49 ...
Chosen

My Definition **Bible Examples**

- [ ] I saw chosen personified
- [ ] I need to work on this
- [ ] This week I nailed it!

- [ ] Women in the Bible
- [ ] My favorite
- [ ] Bible verses

Snapshot of My Week

Week 50 ...
Surrender

My Definition **Bible Examples**

- ☐ I saw surrender personified
- ☐ I need to work on this
- ☐ This week I nailed it!

- ☐ Women in the Bible
- ☐ My favorite
- ☐ Bible verses

Snapshot of My Week

_____

Week 51 ...
Denial

My Definition 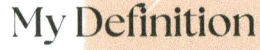 Bible Examples

- ☐ I saw denial personified
- ☐ I need to work on this
- ☐ This week I nailed it!
- ☐ Women in the Bible
- ☐ My favorite
- ☐ Bible verses

Snapshot of My Week

Week 52 ...

Love

My Definition   Bible Examples

- ☐ I saw love personified
- ☐ I need to work on this
- ☐ This week I nailed it!

- ☐ Women in the Bible
- ☐ My favorite
- ☐ Bible verses

Snapshot of My Week

www.ingramcontent.com/pod-product-compliance
Lightning Source LLC
Chambersburg PA
CBHW060935170426
43194CB00026B/2968